MANAGING EMPLOYEES

Series

Recruiting the Best Talent

Pat Brill

PJB Publishing, LLC

Contents

Copyright

Disclaimer

This guide, 'Managing Employees: Recruiting the Best Talent, 'is specifically designed to assist HR professionals and hiring managers like you in increasing the effectiveness of your recruiting efforts. While it may not cover every aspect of recruiting, it does provide valuable tools for finding the best people for your company.

Being well-versed in federal and specific state employment laws is crucial when recruiting. Failure to do so could lead to legal issues that could harm your company. It is highly recommended that you consult an expert for advice tailored to your situation. No book or other published material can replace personalized guidance from an expert. Still, this guide will provide a solid foundation of legal considerations to keep in mind, keeping you alert and attentive in your legal matters.

As different hiring team members complete recruiting, each interviewer will interact with candidates differently. However, the tools offered in this book are not just guidelines but effective strategies designed to guide the process and increase your chances of finding and hiring the best talent for your company. While I cannot guarantee success, I am confident in the effectiveness of these tools, which should reassure you in your recruiting efforts.

Introduction

Recruiting the right talent is critical to the company's success. The goal is to attract enough candidates to apply for the open position and to those who bring the right skills. If you select the wrong person and they don't have the necessary skills or attributes, the business could potentially suffer.

Every person you bring into your company must fit well within the culture of the company and have value for the company's success. Given the critical nature of hiring, having the right tools will help you succeed in this function.

If you hire in haste, you will likely not find the right talent, so take your time to plan your recruiting efforts.

This book will help you avoid recruiting problems and guide you in selecting the right talent for your open position. Identifying, recruiting, and hiring the right talent is essential to ensure a high level of performance from your team. This helps build your career and the success of the company.

Note: There are costs to hiring an employee, and a lousy hire only doubles those costs.

Before You Start

It's helpful to step back and analyze who you are as a recruiter or hiring manager to recruit effectively. Understanding what you bring to the recruiting process can be a journey of growth and learning, leading you to the best talent. Reflect on your past recruiting style and the decisions you made.

- What did you do to get ready for the recruiting process?
- How did you source candidates?
- How did you select the candidates to interview?
- Review how much time you spoke vs. when the candidate spoke in the interview.
- What questions did you have ready for the candidates?
- Did you initially help the candidate feel comfortable, or are you the challenging interviewer? The challenging interviewing style is effective when determining how a candidate handles stress, especially when working with customers.

- Did you take notes during the interview or hope you would remember what they said?
- Were you immediately impressed and stopped asking for more details about their performance? Even if the candidate seems to have all of the right qualifications, complete your list of questions and continue to ask for more information about what they did, how they did it, and what the outcomes were.
- Were you listening to what they said? Did you ask clarifying questions?
- Are you looking for candidates who are more qualified than you? Or are you evaluating the candidates through a funnel to see whether you can control their performance?
- Did you know how much the new hire could add to your bottom line?

The more you understand yourself and your comfort level in recruiting, the better your performance in selecting the right talent for your team will be.

Talent Sourcing

Company's Vision

All companies require a strong vision statement to market their products or services. It is a tool for employees to integrate the company's vision into everything they do. This vision must be the foundation of all your recruiting efforts.

What is your organization's purpose, values, and culture? If you have a completed vision, use that in your recruiting efforts. Ask the candidate questions that will help you decide whether they are high performers and would fit into your culture. For example, if one of the company's values is quality, how is it incorporated into the culture of the organization? Are there metrics or milestones that employees must attain to produce the best quality product or service for the company?

When you know how quality is embedded into your organization, you can ask candidates: "How do you ensure quality is part of your performance? Provide me with details of a project you worked on where you were responsible for the quality of the outcome."

You will interview candidates based on their skills, knowledge, and abilities and whether they fit your company well.

If your company still needs a complete vision, create a purpose, a list of values, and a clear, well-defined statement of its culture so you can communicate these to potential candidates and ensure they are appropriate for your company.

Purpose of the Vision Statement

What is your organization's reason for being? What is the company's focus today, and what do you want to become? The vision statement inspires employees and guides their behavior and performance. Employees are more effective in their performance when they can relate it to the company's vision. It is a guidepost for working for the company. Keeping the vision in front of employees and letting potential candidates know what is essential in the company is critical.

Values

Your company's values will shape your culture. For example, if one of your values is communication and transparency with your employees and customers, how would that value support your purpose?

Employees want and need to know the company's values. Values are the guiding light for leadership and employees to collaborate to create a solid working environment that supports the organization's purpose.

Culture

You must communicate the company's culture throughout the recruiting process. The culture can be shared values, dress code, or virtual versus in-house work environment. Before you start recruiting, ask yourself the following questions and create a clear picture of the right candidate for your company:

- How important are all employees to support the company's purpose and values?
- How will you manage employees according to the company's vision and values?
- Is your organization flat or hierarchical in nature?
- Is your office open, or are there many offices/cubicles where management works?
- Is there diversity in your employee base?
- How does the company celebrate together?
- Are you focused on innovation or fun in all that you do? Perhaps both?
- How do you communicate with all employees? Do you only share with those who need to know, or are you transparent with all employees?

- Do you encourage taking the initiative and expecting employees to make mistakes?

You can ask yourself many questions to understand your company's culture and future goals. If the organizational culture isn't working and there are morale issues, you must address those first to want employees to perform at their best.

Culture is essential to employee performance and company success. It is based on a clear purpose and values communicated in everything you do.

Recruitment Vision

Only when you have a clear company vision, values, and a strong understanding of the culture you want to create can you envision the best candidate for your team? Who are you looking for?

- Do you need innovators or solid performers who will get the job done? Innovators are vital if you are developing new projects or systems in the company. Solid performers pay attention to detail and promptly deliver what needs to be done.
- Are top performers with extensive skills critical to the project's success? Everyone looks for top performers, though not all jobs require this higher level. If you are a software

company, depending on the stage of your software, you could use solid skills. Yet, if you are developing a new product, you want to lay a strong foundation, and employees with top skills are critical to the success of your product.

- What skills are must-haves? What skills are mandatory for this position to do the job effectively within a reasonable timetable?

- Are you open to college grads with a great attitude to learn? Many companies bring on smart people just out of school eager to learn, contribute, and train them to work specifically for their company. Some benefits for this type of hire are that you train them precisely for what you want, employees are usually loyal, given the opportunity to learn and move forward in their careers, and you manage your salary budget by lowering employee costs. When you hire employees, you will train them. You must ensure you have strong talent already working for you so you have the time to train them.

- What communication skills are required in the role? Companies usually want employees to have basic verbal and written communication skills to work with others effectively. However, some positions, such as marketing, require strong communication skills. This is also true for customer service employees. Strong communication skills are not necessary for all positions in the company.

- What do you offer to make them want to work for your company? Know why your company is a great place to work. When you interview a candidate, you want to know about them, but they also sell the company. Highlight all the benefits, whether your benefits, salary, or excellent workplace culture.

- Why do you think candidates will think this is a great place to work? Here is when you highlight the working environment. What is the culture, and why do current employees love working at your company? For example, is it a virtual company where employees can work at home and not commute? Or do you have wacky Fridays where everyone comes together to relax and play? Let the potential candidate know what makes your culture fun, challenging, and respectful.

- Does your recruitment vision include minority, disabled, or multi-generational employees? It's essential to generate applicants from a wide variety of individuals. There are multiple reasons this is an effective recruitment strategy. You enlarge your pool of potential talent and diversify your workforce. Diversity in the workplace helps build more creative and productive employees, potentially strengthening a company's bottom line.

Assessing Position within the Organization

Understand where the available position fits into your organization. When you know how it fits into the company's business needs and how it interacts with others in the organization, you can evaluate its value and appropriately compensate the person.

Suppose it's a critical hire and essential to the company's success. In that case, finding the right talent and understanding the compensation parameters for this role is crucial before you start your search.

Office vs. Virtual Hires

Whether hiring for an in-office or a virtual hire, your job is discovering the best talent for the available position. You may have no choice whether it's an in-office or virtual hire, as all employees might need to come into the office. If your company is flexible, think about finding the best talent to fit your needs.

More and more companies are looking for talent outside their backyard. For example, technical people can work remotely to access all the systems from their homes. If the market is competitive for finding technical talent, you may want to search in other states for your next hire and possibly for a better price.

Before starting a search, decide whether having the person in the office is critical. Know your marketplace and then decide whether you want in-office or virtual employees. The market could be the driver of this decision. When the economy is more robust, employers have the budget to hire technical talent. In a strong economy, the unemployment rate for technical staff is low, which means fewer candidates are looking for jobs. Employers must research market value, create a robust offer package, use recruiters if necessary, and highlight the work challenges to make it attractive to a potential candidate.

Job Description

Your job description should include the essential functions of the role as well as the values of the company. How do you include values? For example, if your company values collaboration, indicate this in the job description. You can add, "Must be comfortable working with others and leading collaborative efforts to bring solutions to the project."

Consistently use all your values in a job description. You can do that as part of the requirements or include a statement in the job description indicating the company's values and how you expect employees to support them.

If you are replacing an employee, review the job description to see if the essential functions have changed. Don't just post the same old job description. Always take the time to refresh a description so you can source the best talent.

Cost of New Hire

Recruiting Time Frame

It takes time to recruit, and many managers might feel they don't have the time to handle all the other business responsibilities they hold during the day. Rather than spending the time upfront to organize the recruiting process, they may jump in to expedite it. Some managers feel they need someone quickly and don't have the time to ensure the recruitment process is in place.

Recruiting for the best talent takes time, and how much time you take to hire depends on the talent you need and who will do the recruiting. If you have one or an outside recruiter, you, the Human Resources Department, can search.

Note: Do market research to understand when to search, interview, and hire a new employee. If the market is very competitive for a specific type of talent, you may need to incorporate that into your time allocation to fill the position. Make your recruiting decisions based on the most current market information.

Before you start a search, you must define the position's essential functions, skills, and attributes that will allow the person to succeed in this role. That's why a job description is a crucial tool to have before starting your search. For more on the structure of a job description, see "Interview Tools: Basic Job Description Format."

Many hiring managers put many "need to haves" in their job descriptions. This is great when you are brainstorming the position. Then, go back and select three essential functions of the position and identify the rest as "nice to haves." Why is this necessary? You want to hire the best talent for the position. If you dilute the job description with too many "need to have," your market is smaller, sometimes non-existent, or you may find the candidate's experience doesn't have the necessary depth in the core areas.

The more tools you have at your disposal when you start the search, the more you will be able to find the right talent and hopefully shorten the time it takes to fill the position.

New Employee Training & Development

Training a new employee takes time. Some positions require more extensive training, which is part of the cost of a new hire. For example, a customer service rep for a technical software company may take longer to train an accounts payable person in the same organization. The cost of the trainers, the manager and coworkers' time, and technology tools will all be associated with them.

Training Consists Of:

- vision of the company
- benefits
- company policies
- specifics on their new responsibilities
- shadowing other employees
- meeting with other departments to understand how the company works at every level
- technology and other company systems
- continuous 1:1 time to ensure the new hire's questions are answered and they are learning and increasing their contributions to the team

Since all new employees require training in the company, its products or services, and how to perform in their new roles, creating a new hire training plan would be ideal. The plan doesn't have to be elaborate; it should be a checklist to ensure the employee is fully integrated into the company.

Break-Even

Some research indicates that it takes approximately six months for a newly hired mid-manager to reach the break-even point and be fully productive. When the employee has reached full productivity, the company sees a return on investment.

For the company to grow, it needs to hire employees to do the work. Though there are costs associated with a new hire, and it takes time to break even before an employee thoroughly performs, the potential for future growth of a strong new hire continues to make the investment worthwhile.

Example: If it takes six months to train a mid-manager, you must account for:

- Employee's salary for the month(s)
- Employee's benefits for the month(s)
- Trainer time costs – manager, co-worker, Human Resources, outside training
- Services provided to new employees to perform their job

Why do you need to know the cost of a new hire? First, budget considerations must be considered. The recruiting and hiring process has direct costs, so you need to ensure there is cash to support the new hire. Depending on the level of the hire, recruiters may want partial payment upfront or within 30 days of the new hire's start date. Other considerations are placing ads, additional salary expenses, and employee benefits.

Second, you must ensure you hire the right person for the position. If you haven't, you could potentially lose the costs surrounding this hire.

When Fully Functioning – Learning Curve

Evaluate each position and assess how long it will take for the new hire to learn their responsibilities and be able to contribute to the business fully. Why is this important? Many business goals are created with the assumption that employees are fully functioning.

If you have a bold goal requiring fast completion, you must hire experienced talent. If you have more time to meet a business goal, you can hire someone with less experience and spend more time training them.

Note: Be realistic when estimating the learning curve. If you say three weeks, add two more weeks to ensure your new hire can meet the position's essential functions. If the position is known and the training time has been scoped out already, you know how long it will take before the person fully functions.

Costs Associated with New Hires

The cost of hiring is more than just a new employee's salary. The upfront costs of finding and training a new employee and additional employer taxes are all part of the total expenses of hiring a new employee. For the company to be profitable, it needs to ensure that all costs increase its value. When you employ strong talent who meets the position's essential functions and is strong after initial training time, they increase the company's value.

Recruiter Fees

There are costs whether you use an internal or external recruiter.

An internal recruiter will cost less, assuming they have the right sources to recruit, can spend the time searching, and are interviewing the right candidates. What are the costs here? Placing ads on job boards, internal recruiter time, interviewing time, and pre-employment testing.

Depending on the job boards you select, the costs can be around $400 to place an ad. If you want to use their resume database, the price could be around $1,000 for 30 days.

Estimate how much time a recruiter will need to sort through all the resumes, interview up to 10 candidates, and organize pre-employment testing if necessary. Pre-employment testing is based on an assessment of the individual's job skills. For example, if you want to evaluate a technology candidate on their expertise in a specific language, some vendors test various types of technology. This way, you can base information on the candidate's skill level.

If an internal recruiter doesn't have enough time to search thoroughly for candidates, the time cost can be significant for your company. So before deciding whether to go with an internal or external recruiter in your recruiting plan, assess how much time the internal recruiter has for your open position.

External recruiter's costs can be 20% to 33% of the first year's salary, depending on the position you are looking to fill. The more senior the position, the higher the percentage. External recruiters are an excellent source to help fill difficult positions requiring a specific candidate package. They are also helpful when the market is competitive.

Manager & Other Interviewers

Human Resources, the Manager, and other vital stakeholders in the company interview most new hires. A stakeholder depends on this person's performance to meet business deliverables.

Managers and other interviewers need to know what the recruiting process will be. If you don't take the time, the process can be drawn out, and in competitive hiring markets, candidates will lose interest and go elsewhere. So, tighten the recruiting process to maximize your efforts in sourcing talent and not carelessly waste interviewers' time.

- How much time will you allocate to the interview process?
- Who will interview the candidates?
- Will there be phone or in-person interviews? Both?
- How can you streamline the time between each candidate's first and final interviews?

Note: Find more informal, fun places to interview candidates in person. Go outside of the typical office environment for your 1:1 interviews. This allows the candidate to relax, and you have the opportunity to evaluate them better.

Ownership of the Recruiting Process

Manager

You, the manager, always own the whole recruiting process, though you can delegate areas of it to others during the initial screening or the interview itself. Why is it essential that you own it?

- This person is going to work on your team.
- They will help you meet business deliverables.
- Your success is dependent on their performance.

Internal and External Recruiters

Internal and external recruiters work with the manager to ensure the best talent is sourced and presented. They advertise the position, screen resumes, and interview candidates.

Candidate Sourcing

The manager usually depends on the internal or external recruiter to attract potential candidates. Since the manager owns the recruiting process, it can be helpful if they discuss with the recruiters what actions will be taken to find talent. How will the recruiter source candidates, where will they post ads, and what are the key functions and skills for the job? Creating a timeline for when the recruiter will give updates and provide candidates for you to review is essential.

Initial Interview Process

Person

The first person to interview the candidate is responsible for presenting the company positively, explaining how the role fits into the company, explaining the key requirements, and speaking with the candidate about their experiences and career goals.

If the company has a Human Resources Department, it is usually the first point of contact with the candidates. The candidate's contact with the company is essential, though the first impression is significant. Even if the candidate is not the right fit for the role, the company brand must build an excellent impression with all candidates.

Suppose the manager is the first point of contact. In that case, assessing the candidate's experience and abilities and building a strong impression of the candidate around the company and why it's a great place to work is essential.

Phone

Phone interviews save time in the interviewing process for both the company and the candidate. The candidate doesn't have to commute to the interview, the company doesn't have to find a suitable interview space, and the interview time is usually shorter as this is the candidate's first evaluation.

A phone interview is a great way to evaluate a potential candidate initially. Use the same questions for each candidate, drill down for further clarity, and listen to their answers to assess their competencies and whether they fit the position's essential functions. By doing this over the phone, the interviewer should be able to eliminate candidates, thus saving the company time doing in-house interviews.

When looking for talent in other parts of the country, the phone, Zoom, and Skype are great tools for interviewing candidates. Using such resources benefits financial costs and reduces time, allowing the company to evaluate the candidate's strengths for the position before their hire.

External Recruiters

What Do You Need from a Recruiter

You're a manager and don't have the time to do all the recruiting for your open position, so you rely on others to help you in your talent search. Whether you depend on your Human Resources Department or outside recruiters to find suitable candidates, knowing what you can expect from them is essential.

> Note: Most companies use external recruiters for difficult-to-fill positions. The cost is high but worth it in a competitive talent marketplace.

Time is essential, and you want to interview strong candidates, so set clear expectations for your recruiter so they provide you with suitable candidates.

A recruiter can do all or part of the recruiting process. It makes your life much easier if they handle most recruiting functions.

Basic Functions of a Recruiter:

- Place ads for the open position
- Sort through the resumes to identify the right candidates
- Use their network to find suitable candidates

- First level interviewing -- screening the candidates
- Skill Testing
- Reference checking
- Offering the job to the candidate

What Else Can You Expect from Your Recruiter?

- That they understand your business. The more knowledge they have about the industry, specifically your business, the more their sourcing efforts will be defined.
- That they provide feedback on the market...what does the market look like, what positions are challenging to find talent for, or how does your salary match the market? They offer different business solutions to meet your hiring needs. For example, they may present a temporary employee who meets the job requirements. They have a rolodex of potential talent that could fit your position well.
- They ask the right questions about the open position.
- Your recruiter can assess the skills of the candidates. For example, knowledge of different technologies, languages, and skills provides stronger candidates for the role. They can be responsible for the whole recruitment process.

What Do You Need to Do?

- Whether you have a job description or not, you need to provide specific information about what skills, knowledge, and attributes you are looking for in the candidates.

- What talent level are you looking for…experienced, highly educated, or junior and willing to train? Each performance level requires a different screening focus.

- Are you looking to fill the position quickly, or do you want the best talent the recruiter can find?

- What advantages can the recruiter share with the candidate about working with you, your department, or the company? Even if it is an inside recruiter, cover this point with them.

- If you have several open positions, determine how the recruiter handles them…equally or focus on the most critical role first.

- State your budget for the position…how much you are willing to pay for the position? If you are looking for top talent, you must pay more.

- For an outside recruiter, you need to negotiate the amount you are willing to pay the recruiter if they locate the right candidate. Payment is usually a percentage of the candidate's annual salary. Recruiting fees range from 20%-35% of the yearly salary. You can expect to be offered a three-month guarantee that the candidate meets the job requirements. If the employee doesn't work out, the recruiter will probably pro-rate the amount they return based on how long the person was in the position. Or they will not return any money and continue to search for a replacement candidate.

You are building a relationship with the recruiter; they are your initial spokesperson for all candidates. They represent you and the company. You don't want to lose a strong candidate because the recruiter didn't present the position correctly. Spend the initial time upfront to ensure the recruiter knows what to do.

Out of Box Thinking (Creative Solutions)

Finding great talent takes time, effort, and creativity. Where do you find the right person who is excellent at the position's essential functions and happy and productive while doing it? Too often, we go to the most apparent places where managers compete with other companies in the industry. Take time to brainstorm with others to develop creative ways to find the right talent.

Have a lunchtime brainstorming session and include all the stakeholders in the position. Each stakeholder depends on this hire to meet their business needs. No suggestion is wrong; instead, have fun, and you may be surprised to find distinctive ways to source or network to find the right candidate.

Note: Be creative, though legal, in your job postings. Make them unique so your company's brand stands out from the others.

Company Website

Your website is a great place to advertise your open positions. Position your Join Our Team section on the main page with a link to your vision, values, and culture and a detailed description of the positions. Your website offers more information about the company than an ad posted on a job board. Use the right keywords for the position in your title, and a person searching the Internet could come upon it.

Constant Recruiting

- Even if you don't have an open position, you may meet someone who could be a potential great employee, so give your card and see if they are willing to learn more about the company.
- Everywhere you go, speak to someone about your open positions if they have valuable contacts.

Disabilities

You are looking for talented candidates for your team. The company will make minor accommodations to allow individuals with disabilities to meet the essential functions of the role.

Email Signature

Most managers communicate via email, so why not advertise every time you send an email about your open position? Your email becomes a marketing tool by highlighting a new position in an email signature. For example, at the bottom of your email, write, "We are looking for great technical talent. Check out our website for more details."

Employee Referrals

Always check in with your employees to see if they know someone who would be great for the open position. Add an incentive as a thank you when they do refer a new employee. If you actively use employees for referrals, develop an Employee Referral Plan so everyone knows what to expect.

Events

Job fairs, trade shows, and community-based events are a great way to showcase your open positions.

Colleges often hold job fairs, a great way to find individuals ready for their first jobs. If you need to fill several positions, you could host your job fair at your company.

Use a trade show booth to meet and talk with potential employees. You or your team members may be members of an industry organization and can use this membership to post or network with others to find employees who have the potential to find talent for your company.

You can also check Meetup.com and find potential candidates at meetups for the specific technology you require. There are many different types of meetups happening all over the country.

Take advantage of your organization to network with potential employees.

Job Boards

- Many companies use major online job boards like LinkedIn, Indeed, Glassdoor, FlexJobs, Wellfound, Nexxt, and Career Builder. If the recruiting is done internally, you must post it on different sites. If you are searching for technology talent, Dice.com is the grandfather of sites focusing on this talent.

- Find the right job boards for the position you are looking for, as potential candidates will search for or leave their resumes on those sites.

Minority Organizations

You want to hire high-quality talent and source candidates from different organizations because it will enlarge your pool of candidates. Reach out to organizations that support minorities to see if you could post an ad or email their membership. Employee diversity adds to creative thinking, brings in more candidates, and indicates the world around us.

Past Employees

Usually, companies have employees who have left for personal reasons but were assets to the company. If their current position is not as satisfying as they had hoped, they may be interested in conversing with you. They can recommend someone to you if they are happy where they are working.

Schools

- Depending on the position, whether part-time or full-time, the schools in your area can potentially provide talent. Colleges provide new employees if you are willing to train.

Technical schools are an excellent source for finding entry-level tech support.

- Maybe you can use interns to fill the position. They will need to be easily trainable to function quickly within the position. Many companies bring in interns and eventually hire them as full-time employees. You gain much knowledge about the intern's performance, which will help you decide if they can continue.

Social Media

LinkedIn, Facebook, and Twitter are the major sites that businesses use to recruit new talent, though popular social media sites are constantly changing. Small sites today can blossom in popularity and become another venue for recruiting talent.

Linkedin.com (a business social media site) is excellent for reaching out to talented individuals who may or may not be actively searching for a new position. A potential candidate is not looking, though your opportunity may spark interest, and they will interview for the position.

Your industry may have specific sites where talent congregates, and presenting your opportunity there would work better for you.

Recruiters are bombarding strong candidates, so if you reach out to the person, put together an attractive offer for the candidate in their next career choice.

Note: If you decide to use this venue to source for qualified candidates or access information on a potential candidate, you need to be aware of the possible legal issues that may crop up in your search. When reviewing the candidate's public postings and accounts, you are given a better picture of them -- you will be aware of the person's age, race, sex, and other "protected characteristics" often part of their online presence.

Recruit with the position's essential functions and stop yourself if you filter people through a protected class. Ask yourself if you are not moving forward with this person because they lacks the experience or knowledge necessary for the position or whether it's their looks or age that impacts your decision. Consult an employment lawyer if you have any concerns.

Tech Meetups

Meetups are a great source of potential candidates if you are looking for technology talent. Just seek out the specific type of technology you are searching for and find out if they will allow you to post about your open position to their members.

For example, if you are looking for a software developer, type the required technology into Google, along with your area, and you will probably see groups already operating with a solid membership.

Women's Organizations

Women's organizations are a great way to find new talent and balance the diversity in your workplace. For example, The National Association of Professional Women, the National Association for Female Executives, and Women in Technology International are excellent recruitment places.

Note: You never know where you will find the right person, so create a recruiting outreach plan to maximize your exposure and find candidates who may not be looking for a new position but are intrigued by what you have to offer.

Resume Review

You will receive lots of resumes and won't be able to read all the details. If your company has an applicant tracking system, you can use keywords to find the best resumes that match your open position. If not, you should review the resumes for experiences that match your open position.

Sort through the resumes, putting them into different piles.

- A - Possible strong match for the position
- B – Not sure
- C - Not a good match for the open position

Go to your "A" pile and start reviewing the resumes. What are you looking for?

- Identify matching objectives. Ensure the objective the candidate includes on their resume matches what you are looking for in your next employee. For example, you are hiring an administrative assistant, and the candidate puts an objective "to find a customer service position." Their objective will indicate whether they are just sending out resumes or tailoring their resume to the posted position.

- Evaluate their skills, languages, and technologies and compare those to your requirements. Besides being a list, see how they used the skills or technology in their work. Some candidates put everything they touched or looked at in their technology area and don't isolate their strongest skills and knowledge.

- Do they have the proper education for the role? Where did they go to school? Do they have any certifications?

- Look to see if there are any gaps in employment. Maybe they were furthering their education, or if not, you need to ask why they were not employed.

- When hiring a college grad, check out their extracurricular experience, which indicates their work character.

- How long did they stay at a job? If they moved around, it doesn't mean it's a deal breaker, but you need to find out why, so include this in your questions to the candidate. Answers will vary and may consist of dips in the economy, relocation, career advancement, or gaining new skills. Their answer will give you a picture of the person's character.

What projects did they work on, and how are their skills and knowledge transferable?

- Were they promoted within a company?
- If they have a very long resume, review it to see if they are robust in writing or have a lengthy career with relevant experience.
- A resume that states what they did and its impact on the project or business is usually strong. Just listing responsibilities doesn't say much.
- Look for strong words such as created, led, managed, or developed.
- If you want to know more about the companies the candidate worked for, go on Linkedin.com and see the caliber of people who work there now.

Note: Resumes are created to showcase the candidate's accomplishments and responsibilities. They don't indicate the candidate's mistakes or failures in their career.

Ensure you have questions addressing areas where they made mistakes in your interview process. For example, "Provide me with a time you make a mistake in your decision-making. What was the issue? How did you handle it? What was the outcome? And what have you learned from it?" This provides you with their processing:

how they handled the problem and if they learned from it. Everyone makes mistakes in their career.

Asking them about their mistakes provides more specific information about their performance. Asking them what their weaknesses are usually elicits more general examples. For example, a standard answer could be, "I work too hard, or I'm a perfectionist. " These answers are bland and don't provide solid information. Instead, everyone has made mistakes in their jobs, so find out what mistake they made, what the issue was, how they rectified the problem, and what they learned from it.

After you have reviewed the resume, you should have several questions you want to ask this candidate.

Now, move on to the next resume in your "A" file and create your questions for that candidate.

There is a chance that after closely evaluating a resume, you will see more strengths or decide that the candidate isn't an "A" candidate.

Note: You must keep a copy of your resume of all candidates you have interviewed for one year. Scan it with the notes if you must refer back to it.

Interview Tools

What is Your Recruiting Format?

There are many ways a manager can approach an interview. Each interviewer has a legitimate style, though you need to understand your style and use your interviewing techniques to learn more about the candidates' strengths, weaknesses, and personalities.

- Make the candidate comfortable – This will help you find the important information and ensure the candidate feels at their best, so their answers give a solid review of what they bring to the table. Also, you want to reduce their anxiety and have an interactive conversation about the company, their skill set, and their desires for their next position.

- Make the candidate a little uncomfortable – This is another more challenging style that allows you to see how the candidate handles immediate stress and works under pressure to make the candidate uncomfortable. For example, a customer service rep may deal with a demanding customer to show how they can handle the pressure. Front-facing company roles such as sales and customer support deal with more pressure-oriented interviewing than other positions.

- Group interviewing—Here, you may have different interviewers with different styles in the same meeting. This can be an effective interviewing tool because everyone simultaneously hears the candidate's answers and can see other parts of the person. If this is a company choice, then it is essential to let the candidate know.

- Peer interviews—A peer in similar roles or equal status within the company usually interacts more with team members than a manager. Peers typically pick up different aspects of a candidate that managers may or may not perceive. For example, a manager may see the person's qualifications, whereas a peer could evaluate whether they will fit the team well.

Job Description

I assume you want to locate the best talent for your open position. In the recruiting process, the job description guides you through the stacks of resumes to find the right candidates to start the interviewing process.

You can also post the job description to attract strong talent. A strong job description helps candidates assess whether the opportunity is a good fit for them.

The job description captures the essential functions of the role, the required qualifications to perform the responsibilities, and where the position fits in the department's structure. To be successful in your search and for a new hire to be successful in their role, be clear about what is expected. A job description is part of the discipline needed to accomplish this effort.

Large companies thoroughly analyze every position within the company. Job descriptions are not just for large companies; they work well within the small company environment. With a job description, smaller companies let potential candidates know they have well-thought-out goals and manage employees and new hires within those goals.

A negative aspect of job descriptions is that managers often add or subtract job responsibilities based on business needs in this fast-paced work environment where job changes occur rapidly. Even so, a job description is still a good tool in your recruiting efforts to communicate the performance expectations for the position.

Job descriptions are also used to evaluate performance at the end of the year. Let's focus on using them as part of the recruiting process.

Basic Job Description Format

Job Title

Location of the Position

Job Status (exempt or nonexempt)

The job status determines how much you pay an individual. It's essential to evaluate the status of a role, as this could evolve into a potential legal issue. The government has criteria that help you determine how to pay an employee.

A potential legal issue is if you have defined a position as exempt and don't pay overtime; in fact, the position meets the requirements for non-exempt. The employee could potentially file a complaint with the US Department of Labor. The department will then initiate an investigation, and if they decide you have defined the position incorrectly, the company will be responsible for back overtime and fines by the US Department of Labor.

Fair Labor Standards Act (FLSA) establishes minimum wage, overtime pay, recordkeeping, and child labor standards, affecting full-time and part-time workers in the private sector and Federal, State, and local governments.

Non-exempt means it is an hourly position and is eligible for overtime. The federal law states you must pay overtime for hours worked over 40 during a week. California has a more stringent overtime eligibility policy, as overtime starts on hours over eight during the day. So check what your specific state's rules are regarding overtime.

Exempt means the position has a specific salary amount, no matter how many hours the individual works during the workweek. For the position to be considered "exempt" from overtime, the role's essential functions must meet criteria tests provided by the FLSA.

Read the Fair Labor Standards Act (FLSA) or check with an employment lawyer if you have further questions regarding the correct status of a position.

An administrative assistant is a great example. This position is usually an hourly wage position. Small companies tend to pay everyone on a salary basis even if their position indicates they are an hourly employee. An hourly position would mean they would be entitled to overtime.

Summary of Position

The Summary of Position section of a job description briefly describes the role's purpose, essential functions, and expected results from the individual filling it.

Essential Functions

Primary responsibilities – describe the essential functions of the job. It's a good idea to estimate the approximate percentage of time of a 40-hour week that the individual will perform each task.

Job qualifications – describe the minimum amount of education, skills, and experience necessary for the individual to perform the tasks. You may want a person with higher education, but if the position doesn't call for additional education, you can't legally refuse to hire an applicant based on education alone.

Before starting the recruiting process, evaluate whether the candidate can perform the essential functions with or without a higher education degree.

Skills—This section provides a basic list of broad-based skills that employers look for in a candidate. Specific technical skills will be listed in this portion of the job description.

You can use this list to form your interviewing questions. Just ask open-ended questions about situations where communication or teamwork would be important. The response will show how the candidate would handle the situation.

You may want to look for skills such as:

- Communication
- Collaboration
- Initiative
- Organization
- Problem Solving
- Creativity

Attributes – list personal characteristics that support the individual's success in this role. A few examples of beneficial attributes might be:

- Ability to deal with pressure
- Commitment
- Presentation
- Adaptability
- Reliability
- Enthusiasm
- Motivation
- Flexibility

Environmental conditions—Here, you describe the physical requirements and environmental factors of working in the position. This may include whether the individual needs to stand all day, lift heavy objects, mix chemicals, etc. If the work environment for this position is based on general office duties, then your conditions would be normal sitting, PC viewing, etc.

The Americans with Disabilities Act (ADA) reviews essential job functions to ensure that individuals with disabilities are not discriminated against. For example, if, with reasonable accommodations, a qualified candidate can complete the job's essential elements, including physical demands, they are to be considered suitable candidates for the position.

Management responsibilities - what is the extent of the person's authority? Also, include a list of other job positions that report to the individual performing this role.

Suggestion - Review your job descriptions whenever you have an open position.

Employment Application

Candidates provide cover letters and resumes, so why would you need to have them complete an employment application?

- An application consistently gathers the same body of information from all candidates. Employers can easily compare applicants' skills and abilities against those of others.

- Gather reasons why an applicant left their previous employment.
- Obtain the applicant's signature, attesting that all statements on the application are accurate and that they understand the policies and procedures of the employer. This signature on an application allows the employer to verify the truth of all the content.
- You could have on the employment application that you are an "at will" employer. "At Will" employment is a term used by U.S. labor law for contractual relationships in which an employer can dismiss an employee for any reason (without an established cause for termination and without warning.) In addition, the employee can also terminate their employment with the company without warning.
- If you conduct a background check, you will need a legal release as part of the application form informing the candidate of their rights.
- Employers must ensure they are not discriminating against any protected class applicants, so asking the same questions helps access the candidate's credentials.
- DON'T use the "box" that asks, "Have you ever been convicted of a crime?" Interview applicants first to eliminate

potential discrimination, and then you can run a more thorough background check.

Note: If you conduct a background check, ensure you are educated on the federal and state laws that address this area. This area is governed by the Federal Trade Commission (FTC) and the Equal Employment Opportunity Commission (EEOC), which enforces federal laws against employment discrimination.

If you decide to use an employment application in your interviewing process, consult an attorney experienced in employment law to evaluate your employment application and ensure that it is legally compliant. For example, California is stringent regarding what you can ask an applicant during the interviewing process.

You should avoid requesting discriminatory information, such as social security data, citizenship, disability, birth date or education dates, and driver's license information, unless driving is a job requirement.

Interviewing Process

- When hiring people, always include others in the hiring process, as your opinion of the candidate is only one view, and other interviewers provide additional perspectives, which could increase the odds of finding the best candidates. Who does the first review of resumes? Each company is different. Most managers prefer having the Human Resources Department or a junior team member do the initial review of resumes. It's essential to highlight precisely what you seek in the initial review.

- Who does the first interview, and how? Decide who does the first interview and in what format – phone, Skype, or person.
- Who is part of the interview process? List all people impacted by this position and have them participate in the interview.

First Interview Agenda

It's good to have an agenda for the first interview that sets the foundation of the interviewing process. For many companies, the internal recruiter will be the one to start interviewing candidates. Setting the tone for the ongoing relationship with the candidate is essential. Here is a potential format for the first interview:

- Reach out to the candidate indicating you want to set up a ½ hour phone conversation to discuss the company, the role, and their experience. Provide them with blocks of time they can schedule their interview and ask the candidate to offer you three (3) ½ hour times that work for them. You are busy interviewing several candidates and need several times from the candidate to eliminate the back and forth of negotiating a time that works with both of your schedules.

- Confirm via email the time you have scheduled for them and provide them with the company's website so they can do their research on the company.
- At the scheduled time, the recruiter calls the candidate and at that time explains the agenda of the call:
  - Spend a few minutes talking about the company
  - Explain the position and how it fits into the company
  - The bulk of the time should be spent discussing the candidates' experience and what they are looking for in their next position. (Have your list of questions ready for the candidate.)
  - Provide time to answer any of the candidate's questions.
  - Get their agreement on the agenda and then proceed with the agenda.
  - First question you ask: "Did you check out the website?" If they didn't do their homework, this will be your first hint on the quality of this candidate. It doesn't mean they automatically failed, but you may need to keep your antennae up regarding the quality of their responses.

Ask the Right Questions

Someone has weeded through hundreds of resumes to create a short list of candidates who potentially meet the position's requirements. Now, it's time to interview the candidates.

What is the most critical component of the interviewing process? Asking the right questions. Most managers wing this part of the interviewing process. They depend on their gut to assess the candidate's appropriateness for the position. When a manager selects this format, they don't delve deeply enough into the candidate's experience and behaviors. In this competitive talent landscape, you can't go by your gut. You need the tools to help you select the right candidate to build your business.

Behavior-Based Interviewing

The purpose of behavior-based interviewing is to discover the candidate's past behavior in a job setting. Past behavior is a strong indicator of future performance. Many companies are now training their internal and external recruiters and managers on this type of interviewing tool.

Suppose you structure your questions to elicit more details on how a candidate handled a specific situation in the past. In that case, you will gain significant information about how they make decisions and their ability to handle the responsibilities in this current role. This is important in assessing the candidate's potential success in your open position.

So, how do you do this thing called behavior-based interviewing? You have two tools that you use…your job description and the candidate's resume. The job description will show you what experience, knowledge, skills, and behaviors are essential in this role. For example, the characteristics you know are critical for success in a particular role might be self-motivation, being a team player, and/or being a strong influencer. You tailor your questions to the candidates based on what is essential to succeed in this position.

Examples:

- Team player means actively providing feedback and prioritizing the team over their success. Some good questions might be, "What does being a good team player mean?" "How do you develop trust with your teammates?" "In today's fast-paced, global, technology world, what attributes of the team are to be most valued?"
- Self-motivation is a tricky trait to interview, yet not impossible. You can ask candidates, "How do you motivate yourself to get work done when it's more difficult than

anticipated, when others are not responding quickly, or when what you have done has failed?" "Can you give me two examples of when you were most motivated in a job? Least motivated? Why do you think that was so?" "Why do you think it turned out this way?" or "What could you have done to achieve a different outcome?"

- A strong influencer demonstrates leadership skills and the ability to persuade others effectively. Influencing does not force others to comply; instead, it uses various skills to join with others and have their commitment to the solution. "What skills do you think are important to influence others? Provide 2 or 3 examples of how you used those skills to influence others and what were the results?"

The second tool is the candidate's resume. Review the candidate's experience and tailor some of your questions to explore their experience further.

Examples:

- Give me an example of when you had to make a split-second decision. What was the outcome of the decision? This example provides you with a greater understanding of how they make decisions. What do they include in their decision-making process to determine the outcome?

- What project do you consider your most tremendous success and why?
- On your resume, you mentioned that you were responsible for specific projects. Explain the scope of the project, your role, some of the significant issues, and how you handled them, and describe the outcome.
- What do you love best about your career so far?
- Tell me a time when you had a demanding customer. What was the issue, how did you handle it, and what was (were) the result(s)?

What information are you listening to in the candidate's response? What was the situation they had to deal with? How did they handle the problem, or what action did they take? What was the outcome of the situation? Did the candidate answer or circumvent the question with information they want you to know about them? This is not an unusual occurrence. Candidates who don't know the answer or haven't the experience will try to position themselves in another light. Sometimes, a candidate rambles in their answers and has difficulty focusing on the question. All are indicators of whether they would meet the position's essential functions.

You will also want to evaluate how they present themselves while answering the question. In in-person interviews, assessing what their body language is telling you. Do you feel they are listening to you? Do they ask questions for clarity, and do they make eye contact?

If you are interviewing on the phone, does the candidate listen before answering, answer clearly, and acknowledge what they know and don't know?

Create your list of questions and leave room for the candidate's answer. Don't write your notes on the candidate's resume…always have a separate sheet and attach it to the resume. Why do you write notes separately? The resume should be clean if another interviewer uses the exact copy and you don't want to influence their perception. In addition, cleaner notes are taken when on a separate page.

Share with the candidate that you take notes. You don't want to make them uncomfortable, but at the same time, we forget many of what candidates say.

If others are also interviewing the candidate, ask them to create their list of questions. At selection time, you can better compare notes and decide on the best candidate to fill the position.

Situational and Problem-Solving Interview

Situational and Problem-Solving interviewing involves having the candidate describe how he or she would solve a problem. Provide them with a scenario in the position you are looking to fill and observe how they understand the problem, what questions they ask you about it, and how they provide potential ways to solve it.

Nondirective Interviewing

Nondirective interviewing, also known as an unstructured interview, is when you ask the candidate very broad questions, and they tell you what they want you to know about them. For example, "Tell me about your work experience?" or "What would you say are your strengths and weaknesses?" The benefit is that the candidate does most of the talking and can be less intimidating in the interviewing process.

Nondirective interviewing isn't usually the best way to fully understand the candidate's experience. However, during the interviewing process, a candidate will share information that is not on your list of questions, and you will want to follow their lead.

Come back to your questions after diverging into other areas to make sure that you have asked the candidate all the questions you have to evaluate whether they are right for the job. You know what is important in this open position as well as the culture of the company, so get answers to your questions.

Another benefit of more structured questions is that they create consistency across the interviews and minimize the potential for discrimination claims.

Read Between the Lines

A candidate's preparation, behaviors, and responses are all part of the assessment process. A candidate's resume and cover letter don't always indicate a person's skills and abilities.

- What makes them a good fit for the position?
- Why are they interviewing for the position?
- What makes this position a good fit for them?

Talk Less, Listen More

The best skill you can have in the interviewing process...listening.

The rule of thumb in recruiting is that the candidate does 80% of the talking. You don't want to be the manager who talks more than the candidate, and if you are, you won't get all the information you need on the candidate to make your best decision.

Why is the 80% rule important? You don't know if you have a great candidate until you listen to them and hear what they say about their experience or plans. Give a summary of the company and the position, then ask questions, listen to their answers, and continue to drill down for greater clarity. Have a real in-depth conversation with them.

While you are listening, you will evaluate their responses. For example:

- Do they answer with specifics or generalities? Do they know the buzzwords instead of answering your specific questions?
- Are they professional in their answers; are they strong, confident, and creative in their decision-making?
- Do they take the time to think about your questions, or have they practiced answers that only partially answer them?
- What are they saying non-verbally? Do they smile, make eye contact with you, and are attentive to you while you are speaking? A candidate can be nervous; this may be okay depending on the role they are applying for. A good interviewer will help the candidate become more comfortable. Yet, you want to ensure they have enough confidence to answer your questions meaningfully. For example, if they are interviewing for a Customer Service position, listening and being composed in their response is essential to help the customer. If a candidate can't relax

during the interviewing process, this could indicate their performance with customers.

- Ask for more detailed answers so you can assess their processing, how they potentially solve issues, and how they work with others. For example, if being part of a team is critical in your work culture, find out how they worked in a team environment before. What worked for them? What were some of the issues they had? How did they contribute to the solution? And how did they collaborate with others?

It's all part of listening to them, hearing what they say and who they are, and then evaluating whether they have the right business or technical skills, knowledge, abilities, and interpersonal skills to be successful in the position and work culture.

Get Past First Impressions

Be careful of the "halo" effect when interviewing the candidate. If your immediate response to the candidate is positive, you may not continue to ask detailed questions. Candidates can be strong in the interviewing process but may not be strong in the actual role. I've seen situations where a candidate was hired, and we soon discovered that the candidate wasn't the right person for the job. We recognized that our interviewing process was not thorough. One way to help get past the "halo" effect is to treat every candidate equally and ask the same questions. Yes, you will drill down precisely into the person's experience, yet your overall question quality will be similar for each candidate.

Sometimes, your first impression of the candidate will not be positive. You will be tempted to dismiss the candidate without knowing if they are a good match. Maybe you judged the person on how they dressed for the interview. Again, be consistent in your interviewing process and ask the candidate the questions created for the position.

Be aware of your biases when interviewing. For example, a candidate graduates from a top school, and you assume they are the right candidate based on their credentials. Always take the time to ask the questions and drill down until satisfied that you understand the candidate's experience and ability to fit into your work culture.

Note: There are legal issues to consider in the interviewing and selection process. You can't decide the appropriateness of a candidate based on their race, age, gender, religion, disability, marital status, or national origin. Your selection decision should be based on their ability to handle the essential functions of the role.

Treat all the candidates the same during the interview process

Evaluation of candidates

Hopefully, you have several candidates that are qualified for the position. What are the next steps?

- Gather all interviewers to discuss the candidates and give their input. This is the time to decide who best fits the role's essential functions. Some interviewers will have concerns, so address them as a team and determine whether the issues are significant enough to bypass this candidate for the role.
- Skills – what specific skills does each candidate bring to the position?
- Knowledge—Evaluate the level of knowledge in their experience and the answers they provided about their various projects.
- Culture fit—What the candidate has said about their previous employment, how people worked together, and what type of work environment they flourish in are all answers that will help you decide who would fit best into your culture.
- Beware of legal issues – did you bypass a candidate because of a disability or other discriminatory selection?
- Reasons for not selecting – write out why you decided against a candidate. This is important in case there is ever a case against the company for discrimination in hiring.

- Reference checking—There are mixed responses to gathering references. Certainly, ask the candidate for at least three references, one of which should be from a past manager and co-workers. However, some companies will not give references or confirm the title and salary unless a release was provided from the past employee.

Legal Considerations When Interviewing

The main objective in recruiting is to obtain information about a candidate's skills, knowledge, and ability to perform the essential function of the role you want to fill. You need to know the federal and state laws that govern what you can legally ask the candidates.

What Can't You Ask

You can't ask questions about religion, race, color, age, marital status, gender, sexual preference, ethnic background, disabilities, or country of origin. Some examples:

- What religious holidays do you observe? Though you are not asking them what religion they are, you can find out what religion they practice when they answer.
- Do you have any children?
- Do you plan to have children?

- Where were you born? Where a person is born can indicate their ethnic background.
- When did you graduate from school?
- How old are you?
- Do you have any disabilities?
- Are you a U.S. citizen?

What Can You Ask

Your questions need to be designed in such a way that you are following the essential functions of the role.

- Are you authorized to work in the U.S.?
- You have to lift to 25 lbs. during your workday. Are you able to do so?
- What days are you available to work?
- Are you over the age of 18?
- What level of education do you have?
- Where did you go to college?
- Travel is part of the role. Do you have any restrictions that may prevent you from meeting this requirement?
- What languages do you speak?
- What is your current address and phone number? Do you have alternative ways to reach you?

- Are you able to perform the essential functions of the role?

Of course, you will ask questions about their skills and knowledge and how those skills were applied in their previous employment.

Pre-Employment Tests

If your position requires pre-employment tests, then make sure to review the U.S. Equal Employment Opportunity Commission (EEOC) on this topic. The test must be necessary to fulfill the essential functions of the job. The focus is to ensure that your testing doesn't discriminate against a particular protected group.

Before initiating pre-employment testing, contact an employment lawyer to ensure that the testing does not discriminate against a protected group.

Background Checking

If you want to include background checking in your recruiting process, make sure you are educated on the federal and state laws that address this area. The Federal Trade Commission (FTC) and the Equal Employment Opportunity Commission (EEOC) enforce federal laws against employment discrimination in this area.

Contact an employment lawyer to ensure you are legal with federal and state laws like pre-employment testing.

Compensation

What is your company's philosophy around compensation? Your philosophy will be based on where you want your salaries to fall within your market. Compensation can include base salary and incentive programs, as well as benefits. All are part of what you may offer a potential candidate.

Understand the Market

It's essential to understand the market you are in because you compete with similar organizations for talent. How do you find the market value for your positions?

You can visit consulting firms that provide extensive salary data for most positions. Small companies don't usually have a compensation team that exclusively researches and fine-tunes salary market data.

If you don't have the money to purchase their data, there are other ways you can informally gather an overview of the market for specific positions. Salary.com, Payscale.com, Glassdoor.com, and Bureau of Labor Statistics (www.bls.gov) are informal sites that provide salary information in geographic areas and positions similar to yours.

Why not have informal conversations with outside recruiters about the market for the talent your company needs? You may ultimately decide to go the external recruiter route, and having early conversations with them will provide the necessary information.

Use the informal salary sites and recruiter information to clarify the salary range in your search.

Philosophy

It's important to know what the company's philosophy is regarding compensation. You want to use your compensation program to attract, motivate, and retain talented employees who will drive the success of the company. Where will your salary be regarding your competition? After gathering salary market data, you have to decide how to compete with others to attract the best talent. Economics, training ability, and critical projects dictate where you want to focus your compensation model:

- Willing to Train Talent - The candidate may have the right attitude even though they may be light on experience
- Looking for Experienced Talent
- Only The Best Talent

Bonus/Incentive Plans

Does your company offer a bonus or incentive plan? If so, it's a great tool in recruiting. It tells the candidate that your company is pushing to grow. The candidate has a chance to make more money and contribute to the company's success.

If done right, it motivates employees, increases company earnings, strengthens employee loyalty, and reduces turnover.

It does take time to create the right plan(s) for the company to ensure that you gain maximum benefits with employee performance.

Commission Plan

Salespeople normally have a commission plan as part of their compensation package. Ideally, the plan is specific, measurable, and doable. Salespeople usually need commissions throughout the year to strive for a higher level of performance, so create a plan that provides income regularly and is closely aligned with their sales targets.

Bonus/Incentive Plan

Lump sum bonuses are usually earned at the end of a specific period and are generally tied to business growth. The candidate can expect specific deliverables supporting his department's goals, which ultimately help the business's goals. This type of plan encourages employees to perform at high productivity levels.

Management Incentives

Managers can be motivated with cash bonuses at the end of the year or stock options. Their incentive has to be specifically tied to their department's deliverables. A performance-based incentive focuses on productivity and accountability.

If you decide to create a bonus/incentive plan for your company, reach out to consultants who can create the right plan. If you create a stock option, explore legal guidance to create a solid plan.

Note: All bonus/incentive/stock options plans must not discriminate against any legally protected class.

Compensation Discussion – Interview

What does the potential candidate want, and what can the company afford for the position? Both sides need to answer this question. Most candidates are uncomfortable answering the question, "What are you looking for in your next compensation package?"

My recommendation is that you have the candidate indicate what they are looking for in their compensation package for several reasons:

- You can assess how comfortable they are about their value and what they have to offer.
- It's essential to know whether the company and the candidate are basically in sync regarding base salary. If they are looking for much more than you are willing to offer for the position, this discrepancy is a problem.
- If they are a great candidate and need a job, they may accept your compensation offer, though they feel they are worth more and will continue to look for a better offer.
- Employees must feel they are being paid what they are worth, whether realistic or not. If you are not in alignment on salary, pass on the candidate and find one who is a better fit.

Note: Unless there is a specific salary for the position, have the candidate express what they are looking for in their compensation. If they ask how much is budgeted for the role, you can answer that you are looking for the best talent. Continue to ask them for a specific compensation range they are looking for in their next position.

Benefits

Most companies offer some benefits to stay competitive for new hires. Potential candidates expect to receive benefits in addition to their salary compensation. It's part of the package offered to potential new hires. Here is a list of benefits that could be provided:

- Health Insurance – medical, dental and vision
- 401K
- Pre-tax benefits – commutation (transit/parking benefit), flex spending, health, dental, vision,
- Time Off – Vacation/Personal/Sick/Holidays
- Stock Options
- Tuition Reimbursement
- Employee Referral
- Wellness Programs
- Perks – discounted movie tickets, cell phone plans, Employee Assistance Program.
- Virtual work

Note: Benefits can add 25% to 40% of the person's base compensation. When you select your benefit offerings, evaluate whether they are the best for your culture and the talent you will hire for your business.

Employee Referral Programs

In this highly competitive market, finding top talent can be a challenge. Employers are searching for successful recruiting methods to bring in the right employees to grow the business. An employee referral program (ERP) can provide you with great talent at a low cost.

It does take some upfront time to create the right program for your company and marketing time to educate the employees on its value. Once you make the initial investment, however, the effectiveness of your recruiting efforts becomes more powerful.

Paybacks of a Referral Program

Employee Referral Program helps you find strong talent by using your employees as recruiters. It is known that referred employees have higher retention rates and increase employee engagement. Do a Google search on "studies on employee referral programs," and you will get a wealth of information on the benefits of hiring and retention:

- Attract strong job candidates – employees are usually careful whom they offer as a referral.
- Involve employees in the company's growth. Your employees are great salespeople; they know the company.
- Employees receive acknowledgment for their involvement.
- Cost-effective—An effective recognition reward pays a "referral fee," much less than outside recruiting firms.

- Decreased time in hiring – since the employee did the initial screening, you can move quickly to see if this candidate is a right fit for the position and the company.
- Retention—There is an indication that employee referral hires have a substantial retention value. This value affects both the existing employee and the new hire from this recruiting program.

Research employee referral programs to create the best program in your workplace.

Create an Employee Referral Process

Set up a process for the employee to submit a referral…keep it simple.

- Design the employee referral program (ERP).
- Create an online system that cuts down on the time it takes the employee, candidate, and company to process the application. If you go manual, have a form the employee must complete, attaching the candidate's resume. Include a question on why the employee recommends the candidate.
- Contact the referral within 48 hours. Employee referrals should be highlighted and fast-tracked through the recruiting process.

- Keep the employee in the loop as to the status of the candidate.
- Thank the employee throughout the process. Recognition is a powerful tool in maintaining interest in this program.
- If the candidate is hired, notify the payroll to pay the existing employee.

Rewards

If employees find a strong candidate, they must be recognized and rewarded for their efforts. As you see, I used to "recognize" and "reward," both of which are important ingredients of a successful employee referral program (ERP).

Most employee programs are not for significant amounts…up to $1,000 per hire, depending on the position. It can be as straightforward or as elaborate as the talent you need to find…do some research when you develop the reward portion of the program.

Marketing the Program

Out of sight, out of mind. These are very true words for some programs that a company initiates. Therefore, keep this program in front of the employee via emails notifying open positions, posting on the intranet, or publicly acknowledging a successful employee as the company's "talent scout."

Have senior leaders become involved in the program's success. We all know that if top management supports a program, the program is likely to get more publicity and recognition. They could recognize all the "talent scouts" at a company meeting and present them with a token of recognition.

Get creative and keep communicating with your employees.

Ongoing Support of the Program

You need to have at least one champion of the program. This individual or department is responsible for keeping the employees up-to-date on the open positions and educating them on the program's value. This education must provide tips for the employee to evaluate potential employees for the company. You want them to refer to candidates that are at least as good as they are or better.

Have a lunchtime seminar. Market it with 500-dollar bills (make-believe) posted everywhere. The dollar bill should reflect the amount you offer for each employee referral. Whatever the amount, peak the employee's interest.

One company put notices in all the bathrooms as most employees visit those rooms each day and would continuously see the flyer.

There are many places an employee can find potential candidates…friends, peers in other companies, professional organizations, or someone they know in another organization who could recommend a likely candidate; it's all about networking. If the employee has a network of contacts, have them use their network to find talent for the company.

Potential Problems with the Program

There are always some issues, even with a great program that benefits the employee and the company.

- You want great talent. To find great talent among your current employees, you must educate them about what you seek. Give them guidelines, or they will refer family and friends who may not be a match for the company.
- Have a policy around hiring friends and family. The referring employee can't be in a supervisory position with a friend or family member, as it could create issues of favoritism.
- One obvious issue is that an employee refers a friend, and that person just isn't right for the position or company. How do you handle this with the employee? Honest feedback around why this person wasn't right for the position.
- Employee refers a potential candidate and never hears back from the Human Resources Department or the manager.

- Too many rules and regulations and the employee will lose interest…keep it simple and effective.
- The reward for finding talent must be effective, or they will not be interested. Do some research and find out what other companies are offering.
- If you don't actively market the program, it will collect dust. This is a definite waste of an excellent recruiting method.

Overall Benefits of the Program

Employee referrals usually have a higher retention rate, and employees are more involved with their work and the team.

Turnover

Why is *turnover* a part of a recruiting book? Suppose you have any turnover in your organization and haven't evaluated the reason for the change. In that case, you may repeat your mistakes and find the wrong talent or bring in great talent who will not be satisfied in your company. Hiring mistakes will happen at times, resulting in turnover that can be costly. What is essential in this process is to understand the reasons why so you can bring in the right talent.

If turnover is mainly based on an employee's decision and not restructuring or downsizing, then take the time to understand why so you can correct the problem and make sure you find the right talent to fill the position.

There are turnover costs, and a business must learn from its mistakes or losses.

People Leaving?

Why

There are many reasons why an employee leaves. Work with your Human Resources Department or manager to better understand why you lost an employee. Some common reasons:

- Employees' relationships with their managers are not working. Maybe the manager is not listening or doesn't hold them accountable. If a manager doesn't treat their employees respectfully, performance will decrease, and employees will leave.
- Not connected to the vision or the big picture of the company. Employees need to feel connected to the company's goals, know when they contribute, and feel successful in their efforts.

- Bored or not challenged in their position. They are not using their skills or knowledge and feel they lack a future.
- Employees don't have enough autonomy and independence and are micromanaged.
- Financial stability of the company.
- Compensation—When an employee leaves, they can potentially gain more in salary than if they stay at a company and receive a raise. Most companies have a specific budget for annual raises. The market is more generous, and new employers recognize this and entice employees away by offering a higher salary.
- Lack of recognition—This is a very significant issue within companies. There isn't enough recognition of employees, and managers can become complacent in their efforts. Managers are either busy, don't know how to recognize employees' contributions, or don't feel employees need consistent acknowledgment for doing their jobs.

Note: Exit interviews are a great way to gather information on why an employee is leaving. Make sure the person conducting the interview is neutral because the exiting employee may be reluctant to be honest. You want as much honesty as you can receive to use this information to change the work environment and recruit a replacement.

The time during which an employee leaves also makes a difference. The Bureau of Labor Statistics indicates that the average length of time an employee stays in their job is 4.4 years. Job-hopping is normal for millennials (1980 – 2000). Technology employees usually have a 4-year window, depending on the market. With technology changing so rapidly, more noticeable job hopping will occur with this talent. This is not to say you can't keep a technical person for longer, though you do need to check in regularly with them to ensure they are challenged and learning new technology.

Still, it is essential to review and analyze why a person is leaving. Internal issues may push people to go, which is why the exit interview is helpful.

Recruiting for Startups

Hiring for a startup is like hiring for any company, though there are some areas you need to think about first before you start your recruiting efforts.

- What is your startup's vision? This is especially important in small companies because you ask potential employees to feel comfortable joining your team. This is their livelihood. You are a tiny company; they want to know you have a strong vision to drive the business's success.

- One of the biggest mistakes a startup company makes is when the Founder hires on their gut. Take the time to create your thoughts around what is essential for the role, the type of person who will best fit into the culture, and how to access the tenacity to work in a startup environment.

- You may be tempted to look for someone with many different skill sets because you are light on employees. It's better to create a simple job description with the essential functions you need this person to perform. For the employee to give you their best, they must clearly define their responsibilities. This will generate better performance. Though you hire a specific skill set, all new hires must know they must be flexible because the company is a dynamic, quickly changing, and demanding business. They need to be willing to learn and contribute to many different levels.

- Create job postings that stand out from the rest. Have your job postings reflect their work, culture, and values, and for the right person, they will be eager to learn, contribute, and grow in a challenging work environment.

- You need to create a compelling pitch and have it ready because you never know when to meet someone who knows someone. Included in your pitch will be the main focus of the business and the background of the founder(s). You are selling yourself and your company at the same time.

- Ideally, searching for someone with previous startup or small business experience would be good. Candidates who have worked at large corporations may not understand nor feel comfortable with the dynamics of a startup. Some individuals are tired of working in large organizations and seeking a different experience in their next career move. You are seeking talent and the right candidate to work well within your culture.

- Usually, startups are looking for individuals who are comfortable with new technology and social media.

- You need talent with an entrepreneurial spirit and strong performers. Not everyone has to be a star; rather, you need someone who has a mix of personality and performance.

- Build a network of people you can contact in the future who may be connected with the perfect person for the job. Reach out and follow individuals on Twitter, LinkedIn, and other social media sites so you can approach them in the future and ask for referrals.

- It is a daily effort to build a company and connect with others in the industry as well as with technology leaders. Who in your network could refer a great candidate?

- If you have a strong candidate, have them come in for the day as part of the interviewing process. This is a great way to see how the individual would perform in the role and whether it fits them well. Hire for talent over experience. Talent will learn all they need to enhance their performance, and they will be creative in the process.
- Try the $500 Bucks Program. Pay $500 to anyone who refers a candidate you hire. This can be a current or past employee, friend of the company, business associate, or former candidate.
- Always send a "thank you" email to candidates applying for the position. When candidates receive an email from you, they will remember the company. They may not be the ideal fit right now, though they could know someone who is a better match for an open position in the future. This is about branding your recruiting efforts.

Alternatives to Recruiting Full-Time Employees

There are other sources for talent to fill the gap in what skills & knowledge you have currently missing in-house. If the need is continuous, consider hiring a person as an employee to fill the role.

Though there are other alternatives, especially if the gap is for a limited time or you need particular skill sets:

- Contract/Consultant – you can outsource the needed skills to a freelancer, outside consultant, or a short-term contract individual. For example, companies outsource their project design needs to specialists experienced in the technology.
- Part-time employees—If you can't find enough work for a full-time position, there are qualified candidates who would consider part-time work.
- Job Sharing—You may be able to find two equally experienced individuals to share one full-time position.
- If you have a team in place and have more work than they can currently complete, you may consider overtime as an option rather than the cost of a new hire. For example, a technical software customer service rep takes several months to train fully. There are direct costs in hiring/training. You may consider just adding more hours to your current employee's timesheet.

Reference Checking

You and your interviewers have chosen the best candidate for the open position.   Before you extend an offer, ask the candidate for references.

Everything you have learned about the candidate has come from your interactions with them, so you receive one overall opinion of their performance and behaviors. Reference checking provides feedback from others, such as managers, peers, or subordinates, regarding the candidate's performance and behaviors at work. This final part of the recruiting process is critical in your final decision.

I've seen situations as a human resources professional where we either didn't do reference checking or were not thorough in the process. In one situation, we hired an individual for our VP, Marketing position and didn't do an education check. When the person was on for three months, we saw that their performance levels were low and that they didn't have the knowledge indicated by their education and experience. Before terminating the person for performance, we did call the schools. We found out they had taken one class there, so they did attend but didn't have the extensive education and degrees indicated on their resume.

Another important benefit of reference checking is gaining more information about the candidate, which can be helpful in managing their performance.

In most cases, during the reference checking process, you don't find the candidate has significantly lied about their work or education. However, they may have embellished their participation in a project.

You are looking for a broader view of the candidate from others in reference checking.

Since reference checking is part of your recruiting process, what must you do to ensure that you have planned and executed the proper protocols to gain the most information about an interested candidate?

- Decide how many references you want the candidate to provide and where they should come from. For example, do you want two managers, two subordinates, and two peer references from executive-level candidates? Instead, ask for references for the last 8-10 years -- all managers, subordinates, and a few peers. Depending on the position level, you may want more or less references. More references are appropriate for an executive position because of their leadership role in the company. One manager and peer may work fine if the candidate applies for an entry-level position.

Keep in mind that every position in the company is important to its overall success, so take the time to get a broader view of all potential new hires.

- Ask the candidate for the names, companies, and numbers of each of the references you want them to provide.

- Gather what you currently know about the person from your notes as well as the other interviewers. Put together a composite of their strengths and weaknesses. Create questions to ask the references around this composite. For example, suppose you assess that the candidate is strong in project management. In that case, you want to find out about the projects they lead, what the strengths and weaknesses of the candidate were in leading the project, and how they interacted with all of the stakeholders.

Candidates usually can't provide references from their current place of employment. So, what happens if they have worked for a long time at one employer, which would limit your ability to access their performance from a manager? If the candidate's current manager is available for a reference, absolutely contact them.

If you can't contact the current manager, check to see if they have another manager who is no longer employed by the company while working there. If all the candidate's managers are still employed at the company, you will have to gather from peers and subordinates who have left the company.

What happens when a company's policy indicates that they don't provide personal references and will only provide basic employment information, such as employment dates, titles, and general responsibilities? This limits your ability to ask in-depth questions about the candidate's performance and behaviors. Again, the candidate will need to provide a manager, subordinate, or peers who are no longer at the company.

Preparing for Reference Calls

Managers should make some reference calls for their potential hires. Why is this important? Again, as previously implied, they work for you, so you need to make sure they are the right person for the role. With two people, such as an internal or external recruiter, along with yourself, both of you will have your perceptions about the feedback on the candidate. If the references are consistent for both checkers, you have a solid overview of the candidate and can assess whether they are the right candidate.

- Using your composite of the candidate, create several questions you want to ask the candidate's references.

- Preface your calls with the statement: This is an important position in my department, so I appreciate you taking the time to answer my questions about the candidate.

- Listen closely to their responses – not only what they say but also what they don't say. Listen to the pauses or hesitation moments, as this could be indicative of a potential issue that the person may be reluctant to share. Be persistent and follow up on those pauses, asking if there were any concerns that you could share about the candidate. You should know now that the person has been with the company for three months and is not performing as well as you need.

- You may think the candidate is perfect for the role, and they may be. When going into the reference checking part of the process, ensure you are open to good and bad news. Don't allow your decision on the candidate to limit your efforts in soliciting the correct feedback from the references. Be open and tenacious in your questions and seek knowledge from others to help you make decisions.

- Make the call, introduce yourself, and confirm if this is a good time to speak. It's important to have the time to have a practical discussion rather than a rushed one.

- Ask them to confirm the working relationship they had together.

- What were the candidate's main responsibilities? What projects or achievements did the candidate achieve? If manager, were they happy? If peers ask if they could share the quality of the work.
- How did the candidate interact with others?
- If they were a manager, how did they hire and handle any staff issues?
- In managing the candidate, what was the best way to encourage or motivate them?
- Did the candidate make any mistakes during their tenure? If so, what and how did they learn from it?
- Can you add anything else that I didn't mention?
- Would you rehire this person?

Note: Some companies have a policy of no personal references. Yet if a manager has good things to say about the candidate, they may indicate in some small way that the person is a good catch. They may not be able to provide in-depth details, though they can still give you a positive response to that person's performance.

If they refuse to provide a reference or forward all references to Human Resources, they could want to cover themselves and not indicate any negative performance issues legally. If it's just one

> manager, check with other managers who could provide feedback on their performance.

Reference Review

Now that you have gathered feedback from various sources on the candidate, it's time to analyze and decide whether this candidate will perform well in this role and succeed at the company.

Gather all of the strong reference feedback and see how it meets the position's requirements. Hopefully, your questions will elicit both strengths and weaknesses.

Evaluate the strengths and see if they fit the essential functions of the role.

Weaknesses aren't necessarily a bad thing. No one is perfect, and you can decide whether you can manage the person effectively to bring out their best performance. For example, one company I worked at had a database programmer who was highly skilled in his ability to create stellar work, yet he never entirely met the deadlines. He always came through with solid, high-quality, executable work but was always a little late. Decision time for you as a manager. Now that you know this about the candidate, can you manage the process, keep the person on schedule, or be willing to be flexible on deadlines for excellent design?

Applicant Acknowledgement Letters

Companies that want to be considered a great workplace usually acknowledge candidates when they send their resumes to the company or interview with a manager. I recommend that you have a system in place to respond to the candidates:

- Send an acknowledgment email indicating receipt of the resume. The note can indicate:

  "We have received your resume. I appreciate your interest in our company. We will review your resume, and if we believe you may be a potential match for the position, we will reach out to you."

- If you interview the candidate and they are not the right fit, always send a note:

  "Thank you for taking the time to speak or meet with us about our open position. Though you have qualifications that meet some of our requirements, we have selected another candidate who is a better fit for the position. We wish you the best in your search."

Making the Job Offer

You and the other interviewers have agreed that a specific candidate fully meets the position's requirements, and you are ready to extend the offer. However, a few questions remain before reaching out to the candidate.

- What salary will be offered?
- Who is going to extend the offer?
- How will it be done – by phone, letter, or person?
- If accepted, when is the start date?
- What if the candidate wants to negotiate base or bonus compensation? This happens in a competitive market, and the candidate weighs several potential offers. Who will handle any potential negotiations? Do you have a set salary range? Can you offer additional benefits or a bonus as an added incentive?

There could be negotiations until the employee shows up on the hire date.

New Hire Onboarding

Your candidate has accepted the offer, and you are ready to start the inclusion process for your company. This process is essential as it immediately engages employees in their new work environment and keeps them excited about their decisions.

New Hire Documents

- Information About the Company—Provide them with information about the company, the organizational chart, and their team.
- Offer Letter—these are the agreed-upon terms captured in a document. It will welcome them to the company, identify their title, clarify their high-level responsibilities, identify their team hierarchy, and list their compensation, benefits, and any other compensation offered in the negotiations. This letter will also indicate that their employment is based on proof of their ability to work in the U.S.
- Provide them with general information on where to report and transportation or parking to the company.

First Day Procedures

- HR Meeting
  - Forms – I9 verification – need to bring identification
  - Benefits
  - Company policies
  - Performance Management System

- Manager Meeting
    - Introduce to the team – have a breakfast, lunch, or end-of-day gathering so the team can meet formally and get to know each other a little.
    - Discuss the new employee's role- This creates clear expectations/accountability.
    - Ongoing Employee Coaching: Weekly 1:1 to ensure the new employee is progressing in learning and performance. Plan a forty-five-day out meeting to follow up with the employee and determine how they are doing. You should also discuss the job and answer any unanswered questions.
    - Ask, "What is the best way to manage you?"
    - Communicate with All Stakeholders of New Hire - Department, Company and Outside Partners

- Buddy Program
    - Designate an employee on the team to reach out to the employee before the first day and introduce themselves.
    - The buddy will give them the lay of the land - restrooms, equipment, cafeteria, and coffee. They might take them to lunch on the first day and answer their questions.

- Onboarding a Virtual Employee
  - Consistent with bringing a new employee on board is essential. Every employee gets the same documentation, whether onsite or virtual.
  - First Meeting – the new employee will still need to meet with HR and their manager
  - Use Chat/Video Online Conferencing or Webinars to introduce employees to company benefits and policies.
  - Face-to-Face Welcome – either bring the employee onsite for the first-day introductions or have a video conferencing set up. Putting faces together with names helps the new employee feel more engaged, and the existing employees will be more inclusive.
  - If a virtual employee's responsibilities intersect with many departments, then break up the meeting times during the first week.
  - Onboarding a virtual employee initially means the manager needs to be proactive in daily & weekly communications to ensure the employee effectively learns and integrates into the company.

Note: Communication is always essential with employees, though communication during the first 45 days is critical. During this period, expectations, performance habits, and the employee's impression of the company's culture are formed. It's part of the whole recruiting mentality. You don't want to lose an employee because you didn't have a strong onboarding process or failed to communicate consistently with them.

Final Assessment

After you hire the employee, step back and review your recruiting process to see what worked and what didn't work. Every recruiting project has something that doesn't quite work, and you can use this information to guide you in your next recruiting effort:

- Did you stay within your recruiting budget?
- How long did it take you to fill the position? Is it normal for this type of open position? If it was longer, analyze what stopped the flow in the process.
- Did the interviewers ask the right questions?
- Did you lose good candidates because the recruiting process was too long?

The quality of your hires is directly tied to the quality of your recruiting efforts.

About the Author

Pat Brill creates empowering coaching connections that build strong and successful managers. From sourcing to hiring and on to effective evaluation and connective communication strategies, Pat brings 20 years of experience directly to your management goals. After earning the highest certification possible in her senior professional Human Resources field, Pat has dedicated her life to inspiring team leaders and managers.

Pat's extensive work with managers of teams and projects of all kinds has given her a unique perspective on what works for a manager's success. Combining her management, leadership, and coaching experience, Pat has broken down the key success strategies she's collected into a new series of up-to-the-minute guides for the professional manager. She believes a successful business and productive team requires flexible, nimble, and practical, not theoretical, interpersonal management strategies. While there has been a lot of information available to team leaders and managers on business systems, what Pat finds is that managers often feel unsupported and unskilled in the "human quotient" elements—communication, connection, and other invaluable skills necessary for building a productive and proactive professional relationship. Nowhere are these interpersonal elements more important than between a manager and their team! In this new series of "virtual coaching" guides, Pat takes the successful methods she's employed in her one-on-one coaching and consulting work and puts them in the palm of your hand! Here, you will find the reenergizing and refocusing strategies you need, whether leading a startup, an established corporate team, or anything in between.

Don't leave your success up to chance, corporate theory, or haphazard processes! With Pat Brill's coaching connection, empower your management transformation to build the best systems possible.

Managing Employees Series

Recruiting the Best Talent

Performance Management: Is It Time to Coach, Counsel, or Terminate

How To Manage Your Time: To Get the Best Results